I AM JEWISH

Personal Reflections Inspired by
the Last Words of Daniel Pearl

TEACHERS' GUIDE

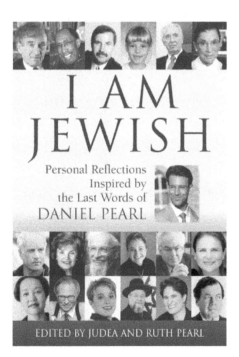

Contents

PREPARED BY SARA L. BLUMSTEIN, MA, MARE
FOR
JEWISH LIGHTS Publishing

I Am Jewish: Personal Reflections Inspired by the Last Words of Daniel Pearl
Teacher's Guide

Sara L. Blumstein is director of educational administration at Central Synagogue in Manhattan. She holds a master's degree in religious education from Hebrew Union College–Jewish Institute of Religion (HUC–JIR) in New York and a master's degree in secondary social studies education from Teachers College, Columbia University. She is a member of the National Association of Temple Educators and serves on the board of the HUC–JIR School of Education Alumni Association.

ISBN 9781683361220 Hardcover
ISBN 9781580232197 Paperback

Manufactured in the United States of America

Published by Jewish Lights Publishing
An imprint of Turner Publishing Company
4507 Charlotte Avenue, Suite 100
Nashville, Tennessee
(615) 255-2665
www.jewishlights.com
www.turnerbookstore.com

LOWER GRADES (3–6)
LESSON PLAN #1

ENDURING UNDERSTANDING

Each person has a personal, special definition of and relationship to Judaism.

FOCUS QUESTIONS

- What does it mean to be Jewish?

- What does Judaism mean to me?

- When and how do I express my Judaism?

ACTIVITY PLAN

Opening Activity: Web Graphic Organizer

On a chalkboard, write, "I am Jewish" in the center of a circle. (See diagram.) Ask students, "What does being Jewish mean to you?" Write all the students' responses as spokes of the circle on the board. Encourage students to brainstorm ideas by reminding them that there is no wrong answer to the question.

Discussion

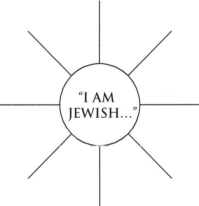

Ask students the following questions:

- Are you proud to be Jewish? Why or why not?
- How do you demonstrate pride in your Judaism?
- Are there times when you are ashamed, embarrassed, or scared to say that you are Jewish? Explain.
- Does your definition of what it means to be Jewish change because of who you are with or where you are? Why? How? (Do you give one definition to your friends at school and another to your grandparents?)

The above questions may be answered by students orally or in written form.

Connection to the Text

Read aloud one or two excerpts from each of the five sections of *I Am Jewish*: Identity, Heritage, Faith, Humanity, and Justice.

    Choose excerpts that are relevant to students based on their ages, interests, knowledge of authors, or other factors. After reading the passages from each section, ask how being Jewish relates to the section of the book from which they read. (For example: Being Jewish shapes one's heritage because it provides a link between generations.)

[The following may be done in a second session.]

Project: Advertise Judaism

In small groups or individually, students should create an advertisement for being Jewish. Each advertisement should include a reference to at least one of the five sections of *I Am Jewish* and should explain how one can express his or her Judaism. Advertisements may take the form of posters, television or radio commercials, or speeches. (The amount of time given to students to develop their advertisements will vary based on the levels and interests of students and the time constraints of the class.)

Presentations

Each individual or group should present their advertisement to the class. Allow time for questions and/or further discussion at the end of the presentations (either after each or at the end of all presentations).

Conclusion: Who Was Daniel Pearl?

Explain the story of the last moments of Daniel Pearl's life to students. (Reveal only details that are appropriate to the ages of students.) Read the first paragraph on page xvii of the Preface. Ask students to explain Daniel Pearl's advertisement for being Jewish.

- How does it compare/contrast to your advertisements?
- What would you have done if you were put into a situation similar to Daniel Pearl's?

Follow-up

Students should interview their parents, grandparents, relatives, and friends and ask them what being Jewish means to them. Students should record the answers from their interviews and determine into which section of the book the response from each person they interviewed would fall. (As in the book *I Am Jewish*, responses may contain more than one theme. Students should assess the responses for one major theme, as the editors did when categorizing the contributions for the book.)

[The following may be done in a third session.]

Students should share and discuss the results of the interviews with their class. Into which category did most people fall?

Create a class version of *I Am Jewish* based on the interviews that students conducted. Distribute it to students, their families, and/or other classes.

UPPER GRADES (6–12) & ADULTS
LESSON PLAN #2

ENDURING UNDERSTANDING

Each person has a personal, special definition of and relationship to Judaism.

FOCUS QUESTIONS

- What does it mean to be Jewish?

- What does Judaism mean to me?

- When and how do I express my Judaism?

ACTIVITY PLAN

Opening Activity: "I Am Jewish ..."

Ask students to complete the attached activity sheet.

Share

Ask for volunteers to share their responses to the opening activity. (You may choose to write the main ideas from students' responses on the board.)

Connection to the Text

Divide the class into five groups. Assign each group one of the following focus areas:

> **Identity**
>
> **Heritage**
>
> **Covenant, Chosenness, and Faith**
>
> **Humanity and Ethnicity**
>
> *Tikkun Olam* **(Repairing the World) and Justice**

In these groups, students should read excerpts from the corresponding section of *I Am Jewish*. (Choose excerpts that are relevant to students based on their ages, interests, knowledge of authors, or other factors. For classes with more time and/or older students, groups can use the entire section of the book as their text.) After reading the text, students should discuss how being Jewish relates to the section of the book from which they read. (For example: Being Jewish shapes one's heritage because it provides a link between generations.)

[The following may be done in a second session.]

Once students have finished discussing the text they should, individually or in groups, prepare brief presentations of their findings for the class. Presentations may take the form of skits, posters, essays, or discussions. (The length and intensity of presentations may vary based upon the amount of time allotted.)

Presentations

Each group should present its findings to the class. Allow time for questions and/or further discussion at the end of the presentations (either after each or at the end of all presentations).

Conclusion

Discuss the following questions with the class:

- When you define your Judaism, do you do so from the perspective of your identity, heritage, faith, ethnicity, or morality? Explain.
- Does your definition of what it means to be Jewish change as a result of who you are with or where you are? Why? How? (Do you give one definition to your friends and another to your family?)
- Are you proud to be Jewish? How do you express this pride or lack of it?

Read the first four paragraphs in the section from the Preface titled "I Am Jewish" on pages xx and xxi of the book. Ask students: What do you think Daniel Pearl meant by his last words? What would you have said if you were in his position?

[The following may be done in a third session.]

Follow-up

Ask each student to write an essay that he or she would add to *I Am Jewish*. Each student should extract a quote from his or her essay to use as its heading and determine into which section of the book his or her essay would fall. (As in the book *I Am Jewish*, essays may contain more than one theme. Each student should assess their contribution for one major theme, as the editors did when categorizing the contributions for the book.) Completed essays can be used to create a class version of *I Am Jewish* that is distributed to students, their families, and/or other classes.

If the lesson is conducted in the beginning of the school year, or in a class with which you will work with older students, collect the essays and return them to students at a later date. Upon returning the essays, ask if each student would write the same essay in light of what he or she has learned or how his or her life has changed since the original essay was written.

ACTIVITY SHEET

"I AM JEWISH..."

Part 1:
Complete the following sentences using words and/or illustrations:

1. When I say "I am Jewish" I mean ...

2. I am Jewish because ...

3. I am Jewish and therefore I ...

4. As a Jewish person, I ...

Part 2:
Answer the following questions:

1. Are you proud to be Jewish? Why or why not?

2. Does your relationship to Judaism change in different situations?
   Explain.

In Jewish Organizations

- As the catalyst and basis for community-wide events involving all streams of Judaism to strengthen community bonds.

In Synagogue Services for High Holy Days, Shabbat and Other Times

- Sermon topic

- *Selichot* theme, *shofarot* theme, Yom Kippur afternoon discussion theme with members of the congregation invited in advance to write their own personal reflections and read them to the congregation as basis for further discussion.

- Topic for outreach/*keruv* programs and membership development programs

- Support material for interfaith services

In Adult Education

- Study material for Jewish identity workshops

- Book club discussions

- Conversion classes

- Promote understanding in interfaith relationships

- Supplement community Passover Seder readings

- Reference material for synagogue libraries

With Teenagers

- Building and strengthening Jewish identity and appreciation of and respect for the diversity of the Jewish People.

  - Confirmation classes, summer camps and youth groups — writing their own reflections and reading them to the group as a basis for further discussion.

  - Bar/Bat Mitzvah gift from the congregation

  - Confirmation gift from the congregation

With Children

- Building and strengthening Jewish identity.

  - Religious/Hebrew School discussions

  - Bar/Bat Mitzvah preparation

  - Family heritage discussions

9 781683 361220